Cornerstones of Freedom

The Lincoln-Douglas Debates

Brendan January

CHILDREN'S PRESS®
A Division of Grolier Publishing
New York • London • Hong Kong • Sydney
Danbury, Connecticut

Library of Congress Cataloging-in-Publication Data

January, Brendan, 1972–
    The Lincoln-Douglas debates / by Brendan January.
      p. cm.—(Cornerstones of freedom)
    Includes index.
    Summary: Describes the seven debates held from August to
October 1858 between Stephen Douglas and Abraham Lincoln who
were campaigning for election as Illinois Senator.
    ISBN: 0-516-20844-6
    1. Lincoln-Douglas debates, 1858—Juvenile literature. [1. Lincoln-
Douglas debates, 1858. 2. Lincoln, Abraham, 1809–1865. 3. Douglas,
Stephen Arnold, 1813–1861.] I. Title. II. Series.
E457.4.J36 1998
973.7'0922—dc21

                  97-9302
                  CIP
                  AC

The present-day site of the Lincoln-Douglas debate in Jonesboro, Illinois

At 1:00 P.M. on Saturday, August 21, 1858, thousands of people crowded into the Ottawa, Illinois, town square. At one end of the square stood a wooden platform decorated with colorful ribbons and flags. Boys climbed into the trees to get a better view of the stage. The crowd buzzed with anticipation. Most of the people there had traveled long distances to hear Abraham Lincoln and Stephen A. Douglas debate for the Illinois senate seat.

An enthusiastic crowd gathered in Ottawa, Illinois, for the first Lincoln-Douglas debate.

The scene in Ottawa was like a festival. Military units marched in formation and fired artillery salutes. Brass bands played concerts on street

Abraham Lincoln

corners. Merchants shouted and displayed their goods for sale. The horse-drawn traffic kicked up choking clouds of dust through the town.

A few minutes after 2:00 P.M., a wave of excitement surged through the crowd. The candidates had appeared! Both men had hundreds of supporters present, and cheers echoed through the square as Lincoln and Douglas walked onto the stage.

Few members of the audience could imagine two men who looked more different. Lincoln's tall and slim body towered above Douglas, who was short and stout. One newspaper reported that Lincoln's height made Douglas look like a dwarf. Lincoln's ill-fitting coat and baggy trousers hung awkwardly on his body. His rumpled stovepipe hat looked ridiculous. Douglas, however, appeared splendid in a handsome blue suit with silver buttons and polished black shoes.

Douglas's rich dress reflected that he was a powerful leader of the Democratic party and was now running for his third term as senator. Despite his height, he could electrify audiences with his fiery speeches. He loved challenges, and throughout his career he never backed down from a fight. The newspapers called him the "Little Giant." In contrast, Abraham Lincoln was virtually unknown outside the state of Illinois. He had served for twelve years in the Illinois state legislature, but only one term in the United States Congress.

Stephen Douglas

Standing next to Douglas, Lincoln appeared very unimportant, and few people in Illinois thought he could actually win the election. Lincoln, however, was a gifted speaker who could argue clearly and logically. Facing Douglas, Lincoln would need all of his debating skills. The candidates would speak about issues that threatened to tear the nation apart. One of the most controversial issues was slavery.

During the first half of the 1800s, the United States became divided over slavery. People in the northern states wanted a society in which people were free to work on farms and in factories. The southern states, however, depended on slaves for most of their labor. Southerners believed that their economy (the way they ran their business) would collapse without slavery.

Slaves, both adults and children, worked from dawn to dusk on plantations such as this, which grew cotton.

Slavery also divided Congress. In 1819 and 1820, northern and southern congressmen fiercely debated whether slavery could expand into the unsettled area just west of the

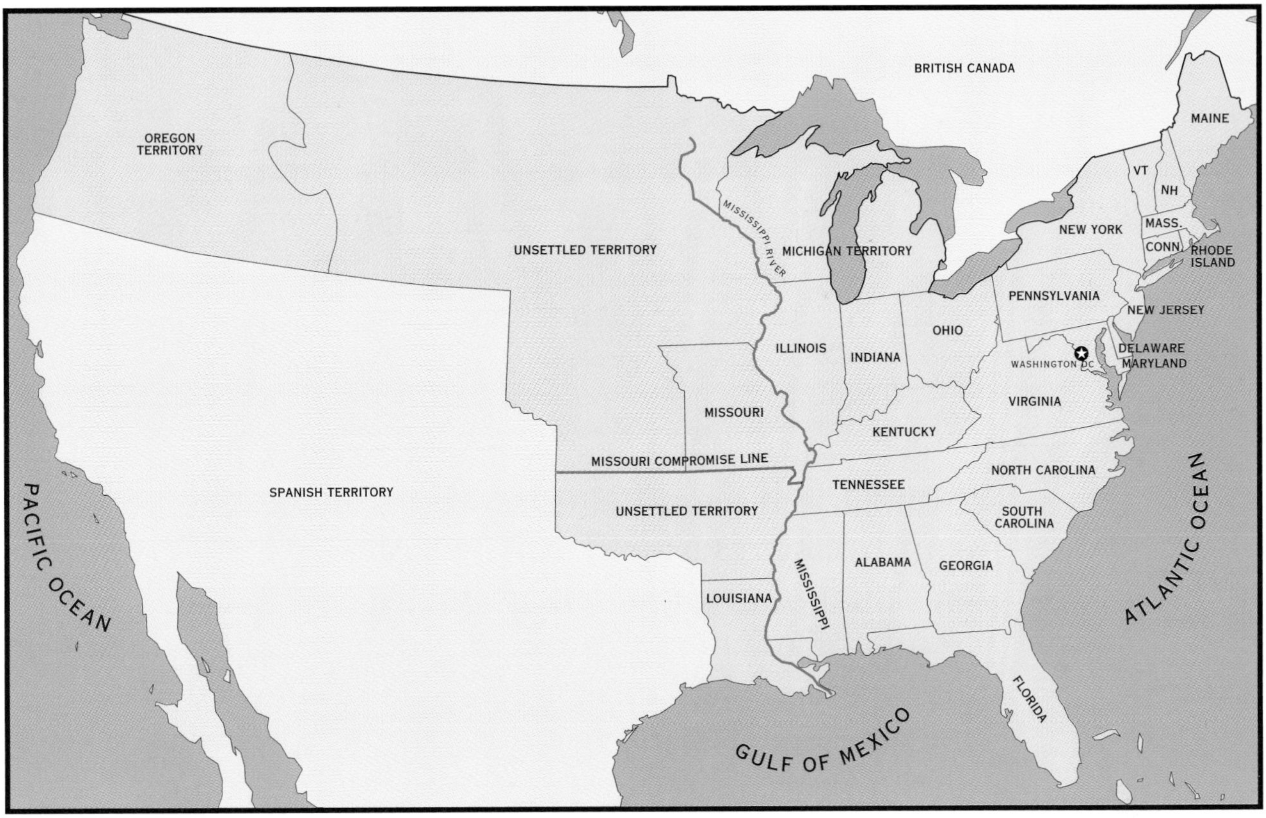
BRITISH CANADA
OREGON TERRITORY
MAINE
VT
NH
MASS.
CONN.
RHODE ISLAND
NEW YORK
UNSETTLED TERRITORY
MISSISSIPPI RIVER
MICHIGAN TERRITORY
PENNSYLVANIA
NEW JERSEY
OHIO
ILLINOIS
INDIANA
DELAWARE
MARYLAND
WASHINGTON DC
VIRGINIA
MISSOURI
KENTUCKY
MISSOURI COMPROMISE LINE
NORTH CAROLINA
TENNESSEE
PACIFIC OCEAN
SPANISH TERRITORY
UNSETTLED TERRITORY
SOUTH CAROLINA
ATLANTIC OCEAN
ALABAMA
GEORGIA
MISSISSIPPI
LOUISIANA
FLORIDA
GULF OF MEXICO

Mississippi River. To halt the bickering, they agreed to the Missouri Compromise. An invisible line was extended westward from Missouri's southern border and divided the unsettled territory (the area that had not yet become a state) into two parts. In the northern part, slavery was banned—no slave owners and their slaves could settle north of the line. The southern part of the territory was opened to slavery. The compromise settled most complaints, and the United States grew peacefully for the next twenty-eight years.

In 1820, the Missouri Compromise settled the issue of the expansion of slavery into unsettled territory.

During the 1840s and 1850s, many northern antislavery societies formed to voice their support for the abolition of slavery.

In the 1840s and 1850s, however, the slavery controversy resurfaced. In 1848, Mexico lost an enormous amount of land to the United States. Southern and northern leaders soon began to argue about whether slavery would be allowed in the new land. Northern antislavery groups, called abolitionists, increased the tension by criticizing the South's dependence on slaves. Although abolitionists were relatively few in number, they pressured Congress to outlaw slavery throughout the United States. Many southerners were outraged by the abolitionists and responded with the assertion that slavery must expand into other territories in order to survive.

In 1854, Senator Stephen A. Douglas proposed a solution to the problem of slave expansion. He suggested that the settlers in the territories should be allowed to decide for themselves. When a territory became a state, the settlers could vote to permit or to ban slavery.

Douglas called his plan "popular sovereignty." "Popular" means that a decision comes directly from the people. "Sovereignty" means the right to make a decision. Douglas proposed that the slavery issue be decided by the people living in each territory. He presented his idea to Congress in a proposal called the Kansas-Nebraska bill.

Douglas's idea, however, violated the Missouri Compromise. The Kansas-Nebraska bill allowed settlers to take slaves beyond the Missouri Compromise line into the Kansas and Nebraska Territories. When the bill passed in 1854, angry crowds gathered throughout the North in protest. A new political party—the Republicans—was formed to oppose the expansion of slavery. Farmers in the North called "free-soilers" vowed to keep Kansas and Nebraska free.

The Republican party was founded in 1854 and held its first state convention in Jackson, Michigan, on July 6, 1854.

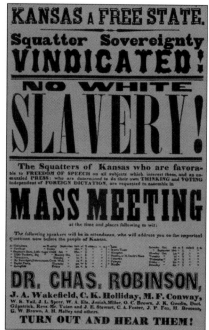

Above: Handbills like this one informed Kansans of huge meetings of free-soilers who wanted to keep slavery out of Kansas.

Right: So much fighting occurred among members of pro-slavery and free-soil groups that Kansas became known as "Bloody Kansas."

Pro-slavery and free-soil groups quickly settled large areas of the Kansas Territory and began to bicker over slavery. As the nation watched in horror, violence and massacres between the two groups bloodied the Kansas countryside. In 1857, two Kansas governments were formed. One favored slavery, and the other opposed it. Each government claimed to be the true expression of the people of Kansas. In Washington, D.C., northern and southern congressmen argued over which Kansas government to recognize. Senator Douglas's popular sovereignty experiment had turned into a national disaster.

While the Kansas situation divided the North and the South, another event shocked the nation. In *Dred Scott v. Sandford,* the United States Supreme Court ruled that slavery could not be outlawed in the territories. Slave owners cheered the decision. Republicans cried with outrage that a conspiracy existed to legalize slavery throughout the nation. They claimed that Douglas and the Democratic party were responsible.

Despite the uproar caused by the events in Kansas and the Dred Scott decision, Douglas ran for reelection to the U.S. Senate in 1858. He faced tough competition from the Republicans, who nominated Abraham Lincoln in June. Lincoln and Douglas had served together in the Illinois legislature. Douglas respected Lincoln's honesty and intelligence. After hearing of Lincoln's nomination, Douglas told a friend, "I shall have my hands full."

In 1846, Dred Scott, a slave, sued his owner in an unsuccessful attempt to be set free.

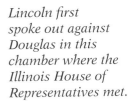

Lincoln first spoke out against Douglas in this chamber where the Illinois House of Representatives met.

In August, with the election only three months away, Lincoln challenged Douglas to fifty debates. At first, Douglas refused. He was favored to win the election and feared that debates would give Lincoln too much attention. But when the

This present-day map of Illinois shows the seven towns where Abraham Lincoln and Stephen Douglas debated: Freeport, Ottawa, Charleston, Jonesboro, Alton, Quincy, and Galesburg.

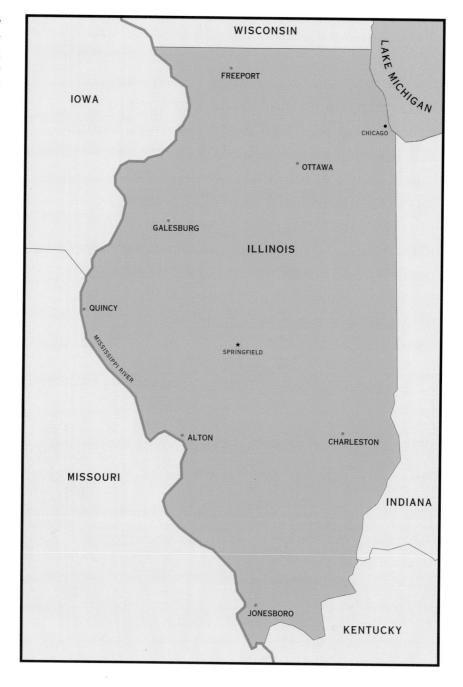

WISCONSIN

LAKE MICHIGAN

FREEPORT

IOWA

CHICAGO

OTTAWA

GALESBURG

ILLINOIS

QUINCY

MISSISSIPPI RIVER

★ SPRINGFIELD

ALTON

CHARLESTON

MISSOURI

INDIANA

JONESBORO

KENTUCKY

Republican newspapers called Douglas a coward, he reluctantly changed his mind.

Douglas insisted on setting the terms of the debates. Instead of fifty meetings, he agreed to debate only seven times. He also picked the seven Illinois cities where the debates would take place. Each debate would last a total of three hours. The first speaker would speak for one hour. The second speaker could respond for up to one hour-and-a-half. To finish, the first speaker could speak again for one half-hour.

The debates drew the attention of the entire nation. Hostility between the North and the South was increasing. In Congress, southern leaders spoke openly of secession (leaving the Union) if slavery was restricted from the western territories. Matching the southern threats, Republicans in the North promised to outlaw popular sovereignty and to halt the spread of slavery. The very structure of the United States was crumbling. A reporter wrote of the Lincoln-Douglas debates: "The battle of the Union is to be fought in Illinois."

As the tension over slavery increased, fighting sometimes erupted among the members of the U.S. Congress.

At 2:30 P.M. on August 21, an hour behind schedule, Stephen Douglas rose to speak in Ottawa, Illinois. Several newspaper reporters waited attentively with sharpened pencils, ready to write down every word Douglas spoke. Within days, the candidates' words would appear in newspapers throughout the country. Microphones had not yet been invented, so the townspeople immediately quieted to hear the speeches.

Douglas drew a deep breath and began his address. He accused Abraham Lincoln and the Republican party of a plot to destroy slavery in

Many historical illustrations of the Lincoln-Douglas debates depict Abraham Lincoln addressing the crowds. Douglas (left of Lincoln), however, was known as a highly effective speaker who was favored to win the election.

the South. Lincoln, he claimed, could only speak for citizens in the North who opposed slavery. Douglas proudly declared that he was well-known and admired by citizens throughout both the North and the South. His ideas, he said, "are the same everywhere. I can proclaim them alike in the north or south, east or west." Douglas's deep voice boomed to all corners of the town square. He strode confidently across the stage and addressed different portions of the audience. When he made an important point he stomped his foot or punched his fist into the air for emphasis. When the people applauded, he bowed gracefully.

Enthusiastic members of the crowd frequently interrupted Douglas's speech with cheers and cries of "Hurrah for Douglas," and "Hit him again!" Lincoln's supporters responded to Douglas by booing him or hissing loudly.

Douglas ignored Lincoln's supporters. Instead, he turned to Lincoln to speak to him directly. Douglas asked why slavery couldn't be a part of the United States forever. State laws that allowed slavery, Douglas declared, can never be abolished (officially ended) except by the states themselves. Many people in the crowd nodded their heads in agreement with Douglas.

When Abraham Lincoln rose to reply, his supporters cheered wildly. Lincoln waited for quiet and began his speech by attacking popular sovereignty. He questioned why Douglas ignored the Missouri Compromise and allowed slaves into Kansas. Douglas had attacked Lincoln for his antislavery positions. Lincoln replied by challenging Douglas's support for slavery, a practice that many northerners considered to be evil and immoral.

Lincoln accused Douglas of a plot to make slavery legal in every state in the Union. Lincoln explained that the writers of the United States Constitution planned for slavery to be restricted to the South. They reasoned that slavery would eventually die out if it was not allowed to spread. But Douglas, popular sovereignty, and the Dred Scott decision threatened this plan. Lincoln claimed that Douglas wanted to make slavery a permanent part of the United States. Unlike Douglas's deep voice, Lincoln's voice was high and shrill. When he made an important point, Lincoln crouched low before jumping up onto his toes with excitement. And Lincoln's bow was clumsy—one newspaper reported that he looked like a jackknife closing.

To great applause, Lincoln sat down as Douglas rose to speak for the last time that afternoon. Douglas called Lincoln's theory a fantasy. Popular sovereignty, Douglas told the

Lincoln proved to be a powerful and persuasive speaker who gained many supporters both inside and outside Illinois.

crowd, would allow the people to make their own laws and would restore peace among the northern and the southern states. Douglas bowed again, and the first debate ended. Cheering supporters put the candidates on their shoulders and carried them through the streets of Ottawa. After a few hours, Lincoln and Douglas returned to their hotels for a well-deserved rest.

Seated in his hotel room, Lincoln discussed the results of the debate with his advisers. Most of them expressed disappointment. They urged Lincoln to be more aggressive through the next six debates, and to vigorously attack Douglas's position on slavery. Lincoln agreed. He was not favored to win the election, so he had to take risks in order to defeat Douglas.

At the next debate on August 27, a crowd of fifteen thousand people jammed into the town of Freeport, Illinois. Shouting spectators gripped signs that read, "All Men Are Created Equal," "Abe the Giant Killer," and "Douglas and Popular Sovereignty." Lincoln and a small group of farmers rode into town on an open wagon

drawn by two horses. Lincoln hoped to make Douglas look like a rich planter who could not understand common people. Douglas reacted to Lincoln's scheme with disgust.

This time, Lincoln spoke first. He challenged Douglas to answer a question: Can the people in the Kansas Territory declare slavery illegal? As Douglas stood to answer, the crowd began to jeer at him. The "Little Giant" stood quietly until he lost his patience and called the crowd a bunch of abolitionists. The crowd only got louder. Shaking with rage, Douglas roared, "I have seen your mobs before, and defy your wrath!" Within moments, Douglas was struck in the shoulder by a half-eaten melon rind.

Republican newspapers carried illustrations that mocked Douglas's size, as well as his supporters.

Despite the interruption, Douglas made one of the most important statements of all the debates. He answered that a territorial government could outlaw slavery because all of the laws are determined by the people in the territory. If the people did not want slavery, they would refuse to accept the laws that make it legal. Douglas's answer was later known as the Freeport Doctrine.

Douglas's response gave Lincoln an advantage. Lincoln asked Douglas how he could be both for and against slavery. Popular sovereignty, Lincoln pointed out, allowed slavery to expand into the Kansas and Nebraska Territories. This pleased the pro-slavery South. But now Douglas stated that a territorial government could abolish slavery. This defied the Dred Scott decision, which guaranteed slavery in the territories. This pleased the antislavery North. Which side was Douglas on?

The entire nation wanted to know. Douglas's own Democratic party was splitting into northern and southern sections. As a leader of the party, Douglas had to be certain that he did not offend either group. Many of his supporters in Illinois believed that slavery could not be forced into a territory. In the South, however, people reacted with anger to Douglas's response. Furious southerners insisted that slavery could not be outlawed in the territories. Douglas found himself trapped by Lincoln's clever questions.

The Freeport debate is remembered for Douglas contradicting his previous statements about the expansion of slavery. It is said that this debate damaged his future political career.

21

The debates continued through September and into October. Almost everywhere the candidates appeared there were fireworks, loud crowds, and celebrations. Lincoln and Douglas took their debates to the Illinois towns of Jonesboro, Charleston, Galesburg, Quincy, Freeport, Alton, and Ottawa.

The Galesburg debate took place on the campus on Knox College, which clearly supported Lincoln. In 1860, Knox College was the first institution of higher learning to grant Lincoln an honorary college degree.

At the Charleston debate, Lincoln told the audience that slavery violated the Declaration of Independence. Lincoln reminded the crowds that the Declaration states "all men are created equal" and wondered how that statement could be true in a country that allowed slavery. Douglas accused Lincoln of favoring black people over white people. Lincoln answered that slaves should be paid for their work, just like everyone else. The crowd listened closely. Most of them were hardworking farmers who believed in work for free people. Few disagreed with Lincoln's statement that slaves should enjoy the same rights guaranteed by the Declaration of Independence: "life, liberty, and the pursuit of happiness."

Reporters continued to write down every word of the debates for publication in the nation's newspapers. (Without televisions or radios, details of the debates were available only in newspapers.) People everywhere eagerly read the accounts of the debates. Across the country, citizens argued for or against the candidates' positions. Both Republican and Democratic leaders paid close attention to each debate. The contest for an Illinois senator's seat had caused a national uproar.

Last Great Discussion.

Let all take notice, that on Friday next, HON. S. A. DOUGLAS and HON. A. LINCOLN, will hold the seventh and closing joint debate of the canvass at this place. We hope the country will turn out, to a man, to hear these gentlemen.

The following programme for the discussion has been decided upon by the Joint Committee appointed by the People's Party Club and the Democratic Club for that purpose.

Arrangements for the 15th inst.

The two Committees—one from each party—heretofore appointed to make arrangements for the public speaking on the 15th inst., met in joint Committee, and the following programme of proceedings was adopted, viz:

1st. The place for said speaking shall be on the east side of City Hall.

2d. The time shall be 1½ o'clock, P. M. on said day.

3d. That Messrs. C. STIGLEMAN and W. T. MILLER be a Committee to erect a platform; also, seats to accommodate ladies.

4th. That Messrs. B. F. BARRY and WILLIAM POST superintend music and salutes.

5th. Messrs. H. G. MCPIKE and W. C. QUIGLEY be a committee having charge of the platform, and reception of ladies, and have power to appoint assistants.

6th. That the reception of Messrs. DOUGLAS and LINCOLN shall be a quiet one, and no public display.

7th. That no banner or motto, except national colors, shall be allowed on the speakers' stand.

On motion, a committee, consisting of Messrs. W. C. QUIGLEY and H. G. MCPIKE, be appointed to publish this programme of proceedings.   W. C. QUIGLEY,
                            H. G. MCPIKE.

ALTON, Oct. 13, 1858.

To the above it should be added that the C. A. & St. Louis Railroad, will, on Friday, carry passengers to and from this city at half its usual rates. Persons can come in on the 10:40 A. M. train, and go out at 6:20 in the evening.

A notice for the last Lincoln-Douglas debate

23

Reporters crowded the platforms on which Lincoln and Douglas stood in order to hear and write down every word of the candidates' speeches for publication in the country's newspapers.

As the debates continued, the basic differences between the two candidates and their parties emerged. Stephen Douglas and the Democratic party believed that a slave was no different from any other piece of property, and the Constitution guarantees every citizen's right to own property.

Douglas felt no concern that slavery might be evil. "I do not care if slavery is voted up or down," he often said.

Abraham Lincoln, however, believed that slavery violated basic human rights. Lincoln and the Republican party did not dare to suggest that slavery be abolished in the South. But they did insist that slavery not be allowed to expand into other territories. The Republicans believed that the United States should be a country where free people could work and enjoy the rewards of their labor.

This 1858 photograph shows a campaign event in front of Lincoln's house in Springfield, Illinois. Lincoln is the tall figure in white to the right of the doorway.

As the election approached, both Lincoln and Douglas returned to their homes exhausted. Together, they had traveled thousands of miles to bring their causes to the people of Illinois. They had given speeches on street corners to small crowds, and long debates in front of thousands of spectators. They had ridden on horses, slept in trains, and sat in uncomfortable wagons. Now, there was nothing either man could do except wait for the votes to be counted.

Election Day, November 2, 1858, was rainy and cold. Despite the weather, thousands of voters in Illinois cast their ballots. But due to election rules, the voters did not vote directly for either Lincoln or Douglas. Instead, they voted for Republican or Democratic representatives. A representative is a person who is chosen to speak or act for others. The people who wanted Lincoln to become a senator voted for the Republican representatives. Those who favored Douglas voted for Democratic representatives. The party that won the most representatives then voted for its candidate. It was a close race. Although Abraham Lincoln received more individual votes than Douglas, the Democrats gained more representatives in the state legislature. As a result, Stephen Douglas was reelected to the United States Senate.

Lincoln was devastated by the loss. He believed that his political career was finished.

When a friend stopped by to comfort him, Lincoln voiced his disappointment, "Well, it hurts too much to laugh, but I'm too big to cry."

Lincoln's political career was far from over. The debates made him well-known throughout the country. He was invited to speak in states across the North. At the Republican presidential convention in 1860, Republican leaders remembered Lincoln's brilliant debates against Douglas. They nominated Lincoln for president of the United States.

Stephen Douglas also hoped to become president in 1860. But

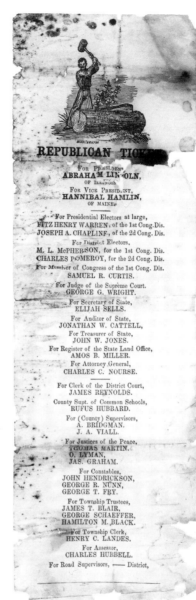

In the election of 1860, the Republican party ticket included Abraham Lincoln for president and Hannibal Hamlin for vice president.

southern Democrats never forgave him for stating that a territorial government could ban slavery. Many southern Democrats refused to support Douglas. Despite their opposition, Douglas decided to run for president. In 1860, the divided Democrats could not defeat Abraham Lincoln.

South Carolina announced its secession from the Union on December 20, 1860.

Lincoln's election to president in November 1860 caused many southern states to secede from the Union. Douglas condemned the secession and visited Lincoln at the White House. After a private conversation, Douglas pledged his support to Lincoln. Douglas made speeches throughout the North, declaring secession to be an act of treason. He urged the country to rally around Lincoln. The travel, however, was too much for Douglas. On June 3, 1861, Douglas collapsed suddenly and died. Out of respect for his old rival, Lincoln ordered all government offices closed, and he received no visitors for the rest of the day.

The legacy of the Lincoln-Douglas debates continues today. At few times in the history of the United States have such critical issues been addressed in such noble and dignified language. With his clear logic and persuasive arguments, Lincoln convinced thousands of citizens that slavery had to be stopped. It could not spread and become

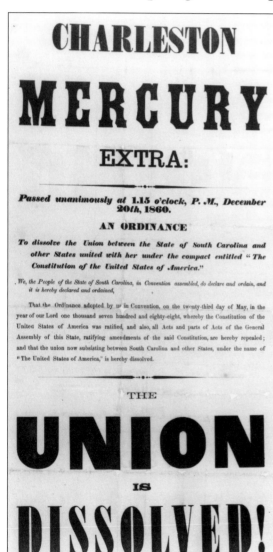

CHARLESTON

MERCURY

EXTRA:

Passed unanimously at 1.15 o'clock, P. M., December 20th, 1860.

AN ORDINANCE

To dissolve the Union between the State of South Carolina and other States united with her under the compact entitled " The Constitution of the United States of America."

We, the People of the State of South Carolina, in Convention assembled, do declare and ordain, and it is hereby declared and ordained,

That the Ordinance adopted by us in Convention, on the twenty-third day of May, in the year of our Lord one thousand seven hundred and eighty-eight, whereby the Constitution of the United States of America was ratified, and also, all Acts and parts of Acts of the General Assembly of this State, ratifying amendments of the said Constitution, are hereby repealed; and that the union now subsisting between South Carolina and other States, under the name of " The United States of America," is hereby dissolved.

THE

UNION

IS

DISSOLVED!

an institution that would curse the United States forever. For the Republican party and the abolitionists, Lincoln's debate speeches demanded that the nation live up to its ideals of freedom and justice for all its citizens.

Today, statues, monuments, and plaques mark the sites in Illinois where Lincoln and Douglas so eloquently defended their positions. These statues stand in Alton, Illinois.

GLOSSARY

compromise

candidate – person who runs for an office

compromise – an agreement that is reached after people with opposing views each give up some of their demands

Congress – the part of the United States government that is responsible for making laws; it is made up of the Senate and the House of Representatives

debate – discussion between two sides with different views

dignified – calm, controlled, or noble

immoral – unfair, without a sense of what is right and what is wrong

institution – well-established custom or tradition

jackknife – large knife with a blade that folds into a handle

legislature – group of people who make or change the laws in a state or country

Lincoln believed that slavery was immoral.

noble – impressive

plantation – a large farm, which usually specializes in growing one specific crop

Supreme Court – the most powerful court in the United States; it consists of nine justices

term – a definite or limited period of time

treason – the betrayal of one's country

TIMELINE

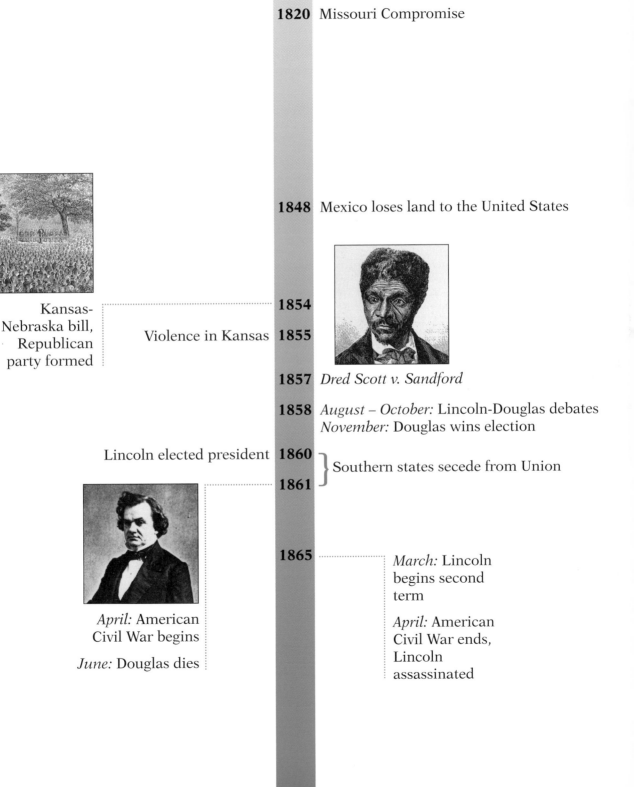

1820 Missouri Compromise

1848 Mexico loses land to the United States

Kansas-
Nebraska bill,   Violence in Kansas   **1854**
Republican   **1855**
party formed

1857 *Dred Scott v. Sandford*

1858 *August – October:* Lincoln-Douglas debates
November: Douglas wins election

Lincoln elected president   **1860**
                            } Southern states secede from Union
                            1861

1865   *March:* Lincoln
            begins second
            term

April: American   *April:* American
Civil War begins   Civil War ends,
                         Lincoln
June: Douglas dies   assassinated

INDEX *(Boldface page numbers indicate illustrations.)*

PHOTO CREDITS

ABOUT THE AUTHOR

Brendan January was born and raised in Pleasantville, New York. He attended Haverford College in Pennsylvania, where he earned his B.A. in History and English. An American history enthusiast, he has written several books for the Cornerstones of Freedom series including, *The Emancipation Proclamation, Fort Sumter,* and *The Dred Scott Decision.* Mr. January divides his time between New York City and Danbury, Connecticut.